ARE YOU MY FAMILY?

MATT REHER - LEAH TROLLER

REPTILES

We all have scales.

SNAKE

TORTOISE

REPTILES

We have claws.

ALLIGATOR

TURTLE

REPTILES

We have eggs like these.

SNAKE

SEA TURTLE

"There is a baby in the egg."

REPTILES

It will get big like this.

Look at my skin.

AMPHIBIANS

We all have skin.

SALAMANDER

TOAD

AMPHIBIANS

We have toes like these.

SALAMANDER

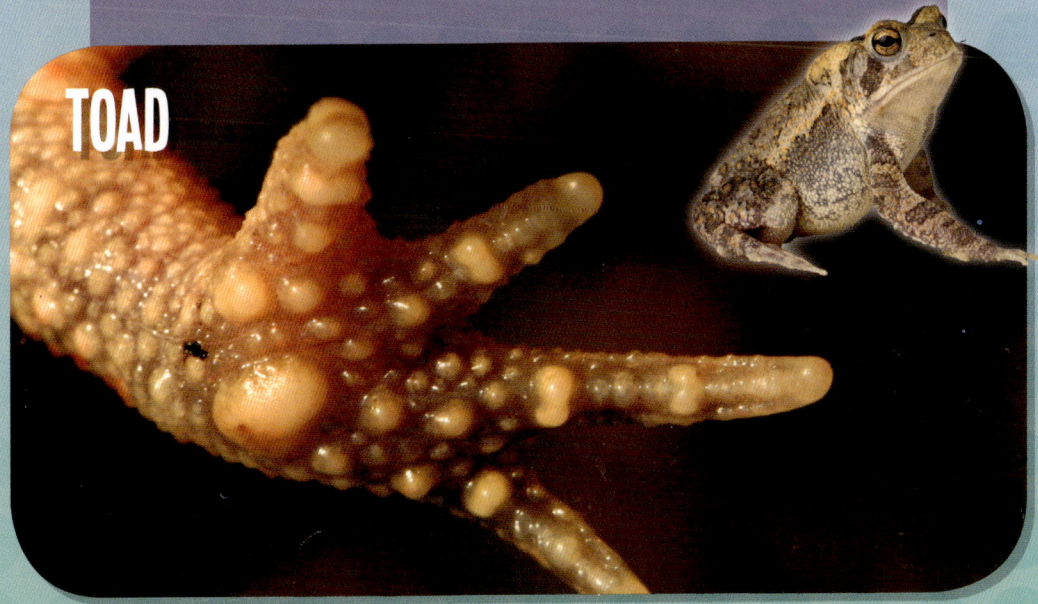

TOAD

AMPHIBIANS

We all have eggs like these.

FROG

SALAMANDER

There is a baby in the egg.

AMPHIBIANS

It will get big like this.

MATCHING

I can use the first letter sound to match the word to the picture.

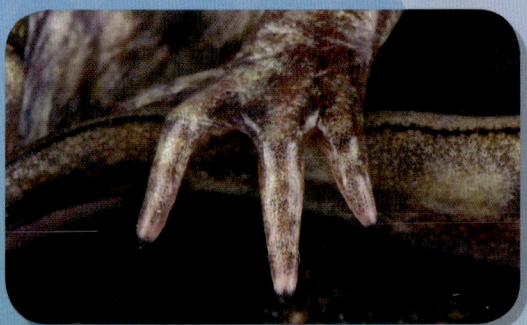

toes   scales
frog   claws

REPTILE OR AMPHIBIAN?
Which family does each animal belong to?

POWER WORDS

How many can you read?

a	I	my
all	in	the
am	is	there
at	it	this
big	like	we
get	look	will
have	me	